About My Life

Montavious Dodson

Copyright © 2014

Children Write Books Publications
 a Division of Nuvo Development, Inc.
Created by Patricia Dixon (*aka Ra Heter Ku-t*)
& Timothy Spear (*aka Mu Skher Aakhu*)

P.O. Box 373015
Decatur, GA 30037

ISBN: 978-0-9719004-2-6

Written by Montavious Dodson
Illustrated by Sakshi Mangal

To My Family

I love to play games with my brother. He said he is going to buy me a game.

My brother and I go places with my uncle. I love spending time with them.

I love to play with my
sister. She teaches me
math. That is why
I know my math.
My sister teaches me
how to read
and write words too.
She shows me love.

My mom lets me go to Ms. Pat's and Mr. Tim's House. Mr. Tim lets me play word games on the computer. Ms. Pat teaches me words I don't know. She got me in camp this Summer.

I like Mr. Thomas.

He is a great teacher.

He loves to take us outside.

Ms. Long likes to get us

at the end of the day.

Sometimes she takes us

to the park and lets us

play football. We have

a lot of fun.

Mr. Turner lets us have parties. He gives us pizza and snacks.

Sometimes when I am at home, I like to watch T.V. in my room. When I see bad things, I turn the channel because it is not good for me.

I love spending time with my dad. When I see him, he gives me money and takes me to dinner. My dad comes to school and pays for field day.

I love my mom. She made me so proud on my birthday. I wore new pants, a new shirt, and new shoes. My mom took me to a restaurant and bought me a toy. It was a great birthday.

I love to play outside with my brothers, cousins, and friends. We have a lot of fun.

I have a lot of people who love me.
I have a great life.
What about your life?

www.ingramcontent.com/pod-product-compliance
Lightning Source LLC
Chambersburg PA
CBHW061121010526
44112CB00024B/2940